IKEBANA
OPPOSITES ATTRACT

stichting
kunstboek

INTEGRATE / DISINTEGRATE

Tory J. Lowitz
USA

SOGETSU

INTRODUCTION

As a child we learn to describe ourselves and the differences in the world using opposites. Like the poles of a magnet, these antithetical concepts define each other and cannot exist without each other. Understanding contrasts, such as 'good and bad' or 'hot and cold', helps keeping us safe and allows us to develop important critical thinking skills. Later in life we often unconsciously look for someone who complements our own character. We strive for what we are not. Opposites attract.

In art history as well we see a continuous movement from one opposite to another: from impressionism to expressionism, from minimalism to maximalism, from realism to surrealism or even abstraction. And the other way around.

Our world is built upon the fusion of opposites going back and forth until they harmonise. Emotions can be compared with a pendulum swinging between extremes. Contrasts, opposites and differences keep life interesting – even though keeping a balance between two opposing forces, such as pleasure and pain, is often difficult, especially when we understand that one cannot be achieved without experiencing the other. During these pandemic years, we have all been confronted with the sometimes-painful balance between freedom and confinement, protecting and exposing, virtual and real.

Floral design, and Ikebana in particular, is often a balancing act in itself. Ikebana arrangements strive for harmony between straight and curved lines, a right balance between taking away and adding elements. These pieces try to find equilibrium between staying true to the shapes of nature and bending and trimming nature's materials to conform to a rule, and between sticking to the rules and breaking them. Opposites Attract uses the concept of opposites and contrasts as a starting point. Starting from a pair of antonyms over 150 Ikebana artists from all over the world made a twin design, two arrangements that perfectly complement each other. The multifaceted ways in which these contrasts were given shape, attest to the creativity and ingenuity of our artists and the sheer versatility of Ikebana.

We are very appreciative and would like to express our heartfelt thanks to all Ikebanists for their never-ending enthusiasm to participate in our books.

IKENOBO

Ono no Imoko, a priest from the Prince Regent's retinue, decided to retreat from active life after three official journeys to the imperial palace in China. He took charge of the Buddhist temple Rokkaku-do in Kyoto and settled in a little house *ike-no-bo* or *cabin by the lake*. Among the things he had learned in China was the art of offering up flowers at religious ceremonies. He started to study the symbolism and meaning of flowers. This is how the history of Ikebana in Japan began. From then on, many priests devoted themselves to the art of flower arranging. During the second half of the 15th century Senkei XII laid down the first rules of the formal upright rikka style, therefore he is regarded as the founder of the Ikenobo school. Autumn 1629 saw the very first Ikenobo exhibition, an event that is still organized every year. Other styles such as nageira, shoka and moribana developed and imported flowers made their entrance. Traditional values and principles are still respected and held in high esteem, but Ikenobo does open itself for influences of modern times. Every style evolves, but sticks to certain rules. Only freestyle Ikenobo offers endless possibilities for arrangements, ranging from natural to abstract.

OHARA

The Ohara school was founded by Unshin Ohara. After a thorough study of Ikenobo he decided to develop a more personal style: moribana. In moribana the flowers are no longer arranged from a central viewpoint, but are designed in the space of an asymmetric triangle. Unshin designed flat dishes for the new style of arranging and introduced the kenzan, a new flower arranging device. This enabled him to integrate the newly imported flowers in the designs. The moribana style was a true revolution. Although there are many subcategories (colour scheme moribana, landscape moribana, upright style, slanting style, etc), Ohara always puts emphasis on the natural shapes of plants and flowers. Observing nature is of paramount importance, as well as the experience of seasonal difference. Rimpa are colourful and decorative arrangements based on the paintings of Korin, bunjin are spontaneous, artistic arrangements – inspired by the paintings and poetry of the 6th century Chinese aristocracy – in which the expressiveness of the piece is more important than the rules.

SOGETSU

This most recent Ikebana school has the greatest number of members in the world. The school was founded in 1927 by Sofu Teshigahara. At the tender age of seven, he was introduced in the art by his father, who had studied many styles of Ikebana. Sofu soon discovered that Ikebana had more possibilities than the styles that had been practiced until then. Ikebana arrangements had always been displayed in a tokonoma. Sofu saw enormous potential in placing it in every interior. His Sogetsu school believes that anyone can arrange Ikebana anywhere, and with almost anything. Ikebana should be part of a lifestyle to be appreciated by many people, rather than being considered an exclusive art to be enjoyed by few. In the beginning, he cast off all Ikebana rules, but gradually understood how rules were necessary to guide students so that they eventually could be given the freedom of interpretation that is typical of Sogetsu. Just as people are different from each other, Sogetsu encourages Ikebana students to be individual and imaginative.

ICHIYO

The Ichiyo school was founded in 1937 by Meikof Kasuya and his sister Ichiyo. They tried to adapt Ikebana to the modern way of living while retaining traditions, inheritances and rules. In 1983, the third son of Meikof Kasuya; Akihiro, became the third Iemoto of the school. In big stage shows he demonstrated balancing and tension techniques – enabling new and unseen possibilities with flower materials. He urged students to use mainly natural materials and to consider the plant's character, the seasons and the positioning of the arrangement. Ichiyo School encourages personal interpretation. Imagination is considered as essential to creative designs as materials and containers. If flower arranging is to be truly fulfilling, it should be a reflection of oneself.

ADVISORY TEAM

Els Claes - Belgium - IKENOBO
Els Claes first discovered Ikenobo and Ikebana when visiting the 1997 exhibition of Ikenobo and Ohara at the Botanic Gardens Meise, Belgium. This is where she met Lia De Grave (Senior Professor of Ikenobo Ikebana - Junkatoku) which she, since that moment, is honoured to have as her teacher. During her first trip to Japan in 2002 she visited a lot of cultural places as well as the large autumn exhibition at the Ikenobo Headquarters. Her passion for Ikebana, the Japanese culture and art only grew stronger. From 2003 onwards she regularly participated in different seminars in Europe and contributed to various exhibitions. Driven by her enthusiasm and encouraged by her professors, she started taking lessons at the Ikenobo Headquarters in Kyoto in 2006. Since then she tries to visit Japan whenever the opportunity is offered and undertakes study trips to the Headquarters to broaden her skills and improve her understanding of the art. In 2016 Els organised large events and exhibitions celebrating the 150th anniversary of diplomatic relations and friendship between Japan and Belgium. Els teaches in the Arboretum of Kalmthout and gives workshops at the Japanese Garden of Hasselt. Beginning of 2017 she received the grade of Sokakan (Professor of Ikebana, 2nd Grade). Since April 2022 she is leader of the Ikenobo Belgium Study Group. Professionally Els works as a landscape architect in the Antwerp based office of Fondu landscape architects.

Esther Hoogland - the Netherlands - SOGETSU
In 1992 Esther first started taking Ikebana lessons with Peggy Maas. From 1994 until now she had been studying with Anke Verhoeven. The beauty of lines and space combined with working with flowers was love at first site. The endless possibilities of creating and the wide range of techniques within the Sogetsu curriculum made it even more interesting. Anke Verhoeven has stimulated her to look at the principles of other art forms and the similarities between these and Ikebana. Because of her interest in Japanese culture and Ikebana, Esther became a member of the Dutch Ikebana Society (Nederlandse Ikebana Vereniging). She has held various positions on the board of the Utrecht regional chapter since 2001 and on the main board since 2004. She currently chairs the main board. Esther Hoogland has also served on committees responsible for organising Ikebana exhibitions and seminars for the NIV and the Sogetsu Branch of the Netherlands. To broaden her view and improve techniques she has been taking lessons with Els Goos and Nicole Kruimel-Rosselle. Since her graduation as Sogetsu teacher, she has given lessons, workshops, lectures and demonstrations in Belgium, Germany and the Netherlands.

Mit Ingelaere-Brandt - Belgium - SOGETSU
Mit Ingelaere-Brandt is one of the driving forces behind the flourishing Ikebana scene in Belgium. She took the first grade Sogetsu in 1979. From then on she continued to gain higher grades. Mit teaches Sogetsu, organizes exhibitions and has been involved in sculpting and painting. These fields strongly influence her artistic work. For several years Mit followed courses and master classes with Geordie Davidson, she also took seminars and workshops with Tetsunori Kawana and other Land Art artists such as Helen Escobedo (Mexico) and Bob Verschueren (Belgium). In June 2011 Mit was appointed president of Ikebana International Belgium, a demanding task that made her travel extensively and made her a passionate advocate

for the further promotion and development of Ikebana. She has been giving demonstrations in the USA, Mexico, Canada and all around Europe. For a number of years, Mit has been practicing sumi-e, Japanese ink painting, which helps her observe and understand nature even better and thus complements arranging Ikebana. Over the years Mit Ingelaere-Brandt has been involved in many of Stichting Kunstboek's publications on Ikebana.

Jeroen Vermaas - the Netherlands - ICHIYO
Jeroen Vermaas started taking Ichiyo lessons in 2000 with Master Corrie van der Meer-Fischer. In 2022, he received the 9th degree of Master Ichiyo School of Ikebana. On this occasion he was also appointed President of the The Netherlands Chapter. He gained a lot of experience by assisting the late Iemoto Akihiro Kasuya on stage during demonstrations in France and the Netherlands. He also assisted Iemoto Naohiro Kasuya during the 9th European Regional Conference of Ikebana International in Bruges in 2018 and was part of the assisting group on the occasion of the Grand Exhibition Japonisme at the House of Culture of Japan in Paris 2019. Jeroen gives lessons, workshops and demonstrations in the Netherlands and abroad. He is board member of Chapter 215 of Ikebana International, as well as member of a regional section of the Dutch Ikebana Society. He is an ardent promoter of Ikebana in Holland and a well-known Ikebana artist.

Atsuko Bersma - Japan/Belgium - SOGETSU
Atsuko Bersma was born in Yokohama (Japan) and started taking Ikebana lessons at the age of 11. Since 1970, she has combined her studies with teaching Sogetsu-style Ikebana in the various places she has lived around the world. Atsuko founded the Ikebana International Hana Chapter of Belgium and was its first president (1996-2000). She was chairperson of the Study Group Sogetsu Azalea in Belgium from 2001 to 2009. She has given many demonstrations and workshops in Japan and throughout Europe and holds annual exhibitions with her students. She has been the recipient of Sogetsu Overseas awards in 2003, 2007 and 2017. In 2017, she also received an official Commendation from the Japanese Foreign Minister, and in 2019 received a medal of the Order of the Rising Sun with Gold and Silver Rays for her merits in spreading Japanese culture around the world.

We would also like to express our special thanks to Mrs **Ivy Le Maguer** (France) for her help and advice in selecting the Ikenobo arrangements.

SELECTION

WATER/FIRE
COMPLEX/SIMPLE
ROUGH/SMOOTH
PRESENT/PAST
FRESH/DRY
FALL/RISE
LIFE/DEATH
SOUL/BODY
STATIC/DYNAMIC
HEAVY/LIGHT
STRONG/TENDER

CHAOS / HARMONY

Martha Bachmann
Switzerland

KAGEI ADACHI RYU

YOUNG / OLD

Denise Adriaensen
Belgium

OHARA

GROUP / INDIVIDUAL

Rica Arai
France

SOGETSU

QUIETNESS / TURMOIL

Paola Belfiore
Italy

SOGETSU

MASCULINE / FEMININE

Atsuko Bersma
Belgium/Japan

SOGETSU

HEAVY / LIGHT

Ilse Beunen
Belgium

SOGETSU

COMPLEX / SIMPLE

Alka Bhargava
USA

ICHIYO

CAPTURED / FREE

Alie Bos-Praamstra
the Netherlands

SOGETSU

AMIABLE / CAPRICIOUS

Jean Brouwers
the Netherlands

SOGETSU

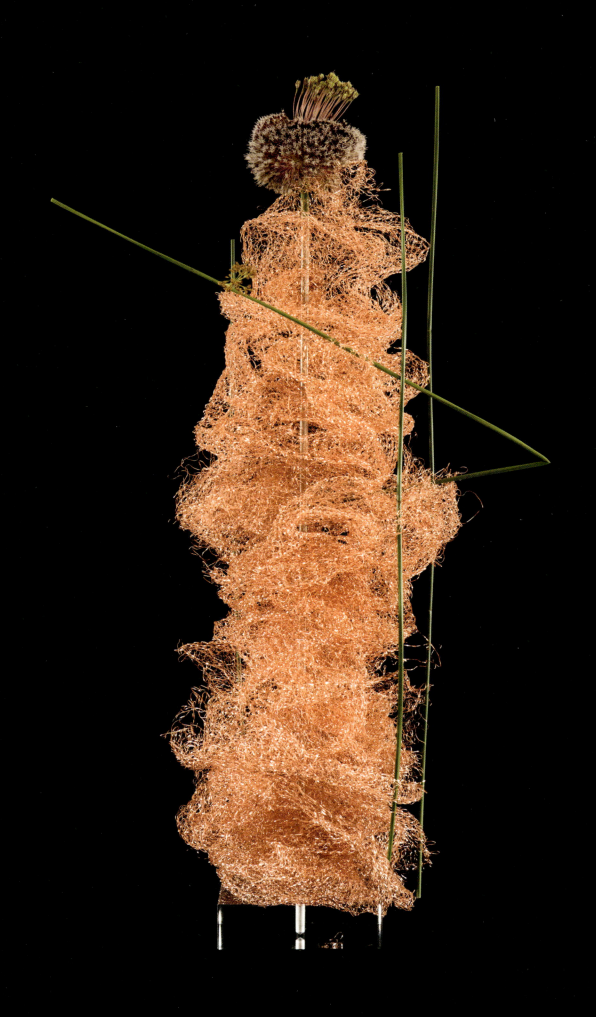

GEISHA / SAMOURAI

Mieke Bruynooghe - Van Elslande
Belgium

SOGETSU

ANGULAR / ROUNDED

Brigitta Buse
Germany

SOGETSU

CURVED / ANGULAR

Elizabeth Campbell
USA

ICHIYO

LIFE / DEATH

Christophe Capdeville
France

ICHIYO

CURVED / ANGULAR

Evangeline Y. Cheng
Philippines

SOGETSU

DEFIANT / SUBMISSIVE

Els Claes
Belgium

IKENOBO

DECAY / PERKINESS

Zilá Da Costa Raymundo
Brazil

SOGETSU

CONNECT / SEPARATE

Elin Dahlin
Sweden

SOGETSU

EXTROVERT / INTROVERT

Anna Maria De Carvalho
Switzerland

MISHO-RYU

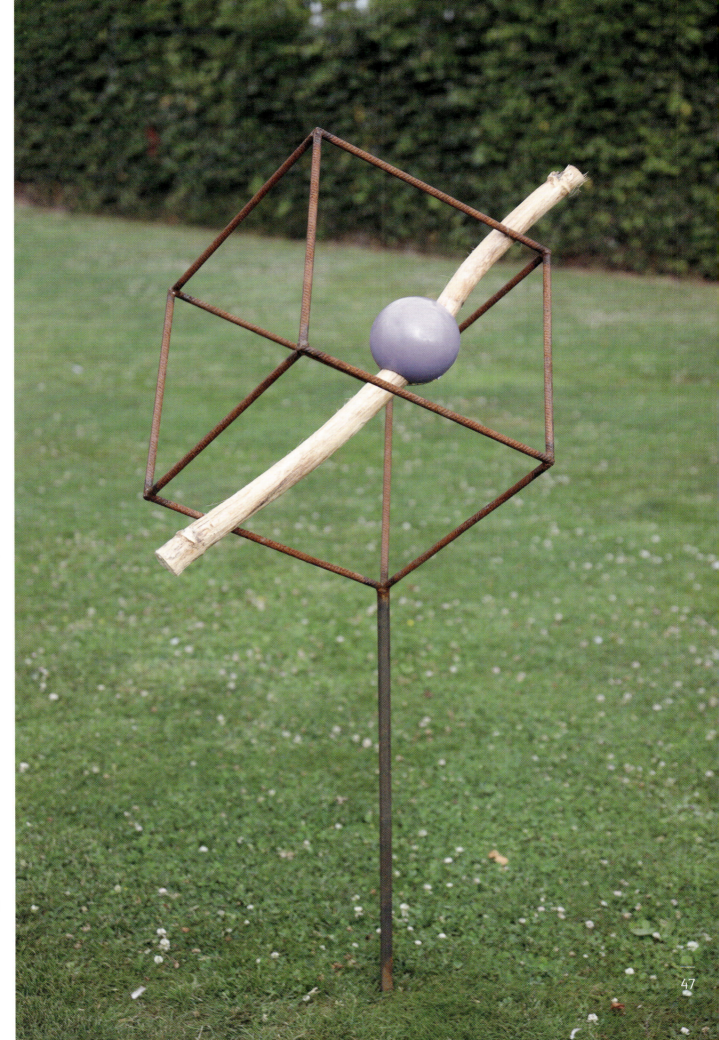

DYNAMIC / STATIC

Wil de Theije
the Netherlands

SOGETSU

ANGULAR / ROUND

Angelika Denig
Germany

SOGETSU

FREED / LOCKED-UP

Brigitte Depienne
Belgium

SOGETSU

LIFE / DEATH

Claire Devleminckx
Belgium

SOGETSU

MEAT LOVER / VEGETARIAN

Rita Dollberg
Germany

SOGETSU

UNRAVELED / INTERTWINED

Christine Donck Guelton
USA

SOGETSU

WITH / WITHOUT

Damien Dufour
France

OHARA

CONFINED / FREE

Christl Dullenkopf
Germany

SOGETSU

HELLO / GOODBYE

Valerie Eccleston
USA

ICHIYO

ABSORPTION / REFLECTION

Alexander Evans
Australia

SOGETSU

SIMPLE / COMPLICATED

Huda Fallaha
Jordan

SOGETSU

TIMELESS BEAUTY / WABI SABI

Yi-Li Fang
Taiwan

IKENOBO

CULTURE / NATURE

Farah Fazrina Rauf
Malaysia

SOGETSU

FRESH / NOBLE

Esther Feucht
Switzerland

MISHO-RYU

EMERGE / DECLINE

Maude Freymond Wanner
Australia

SOGETSU

LIQUID / SOLID

Ursina Früh
Switzerland

MISHO-RYU

FRIVOLOUS / SERIOUS

Lucienne Girardbille
France

IKENOBO

PAST / PRESENT

Irene Gomulka
USA

SOGETSU

OPEN / CLOSED
Ayako Graefe
Germany

SOGETSU

VIGOROUS / FRAGILE

Herbert Grünsteidl
Austria

SOGETSU

BREAKABLE / UNBREAKABLE
BRIGHT / DARK

Fatima Hanke
Germany

SOGETSU

COMPLETE / BROKEN

Mechtild Hartz-Riemann
Germany

SOGETSU

ROUND / ANGULAR

Edelgard Herwald
Germany

SOGETSU

YOUNG / OLD

Esther Hoogland
the Netherlands

SOGETSU

LOVE / HATE

Marilyn Hoskins
USA

ICHIYO

FIRST SUN OF SUMMER /
LAST LIGHT OF WINTER

Jeanne Houlton
USA

ICHIYO

JOY / SADNESS

Misha Huurman
the Netherlands

SOGETSU

DAY / NIGHT

Ikenobo Swiss Central Chapter: Chaoyu Du and Shunzuen Suzue Rother-Nakaya
Switzerland

IKENOBO

SUNNY SIDE / SHADOW SIDE

Mit Ingelaere-Brandt
Belgium

SOGETSU

UPWARD / DOWNWARD

Elaine Jo
USA

ICHIYO

SELF-CONFIDENT / UNSURE

Gisela Jost
Germany

SOGETSU

SOUL / BODY

Elena Karetko
Russia

SOGETSU

EARTH / HEAVEN

Irene Kho-Chen
the Netherlands

OHARA

DRY / WET

Elena Kilchevskaya
Russia

SOGETSU

FREEDOM / OPPRESSION

Antje Klatt
Germany

SOGETSU

DAY / NIGHT

Iryna Korol Latorre
USA

ICHIYO

HEAVY / LIGHT

Nicole Kruimel-Rosselle
the Netherlands

SOGETSU

LONELINESS / SECURENESS

Iris Kuhn
Austria

ICHIYO

FIRE / ICE

Kathy LaDuke
USA

ICHIYO

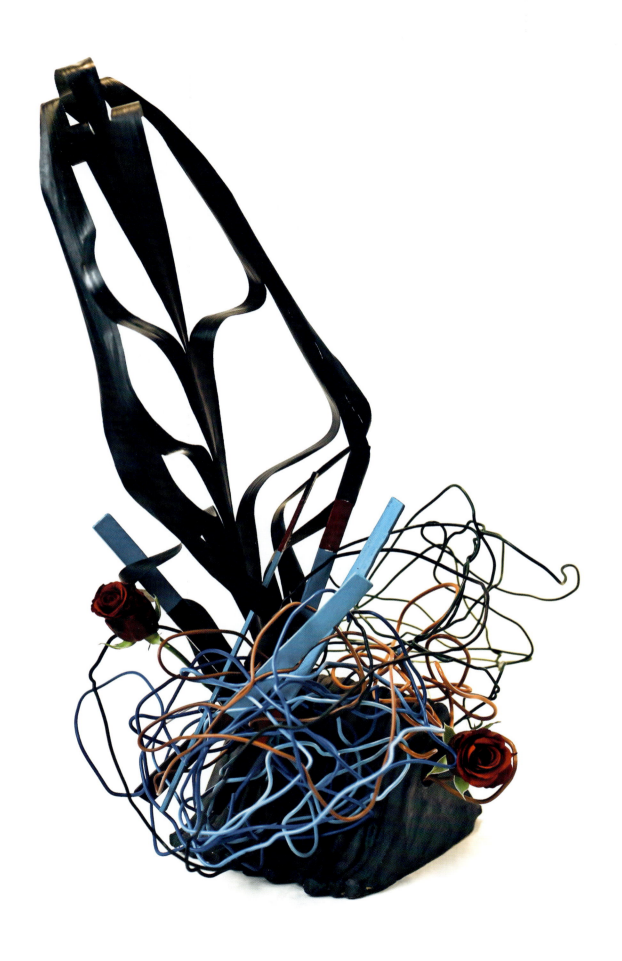

LOUD / SILENT

Tanja Lähteenmäki
Finland

SOGETSU

129

CONFINEMENT / FREEDOM

Marcia Lamrock
Australia

SOGETSU

YIN / YANG

Marta Lanfranco
Italy

WAFU KAI

LIGHT / SHADOW

Hélène Lanz
Germany

SOGETSU

CLASSICAL / MODERN

Ivy Le Maguer
France

IKENOBO

137

MODESTY / PRIDE

Zoo-Lan Lee-Rötter
Germany

OHARA

OLD / YOUNG

Verdy Leung
Hong Kong

IKENOBO

NORTH / SOUTH

Gisele Leuther
Germany

OHARA

DESTROYED / RECREATED

Hedda Lintner
Germany

SOGETSU

145

YIN / YANG

Pat Mackie
Australia

SOGETSU

LEFT / RIGHT

Regula Maier
Switzerland

MISHO

SHARP / SOFT

Milla Mäkinen
Finland

SOGETSU

MOTION / STILLNESS

Rumiko Manako
Japan/France

IKENOBO

BLISS / ANGUISH

Inès Massin
Switzerland

SOGETSU

COMPACT / AIRY

Gerda Matthees
Belgium

SOGETSU

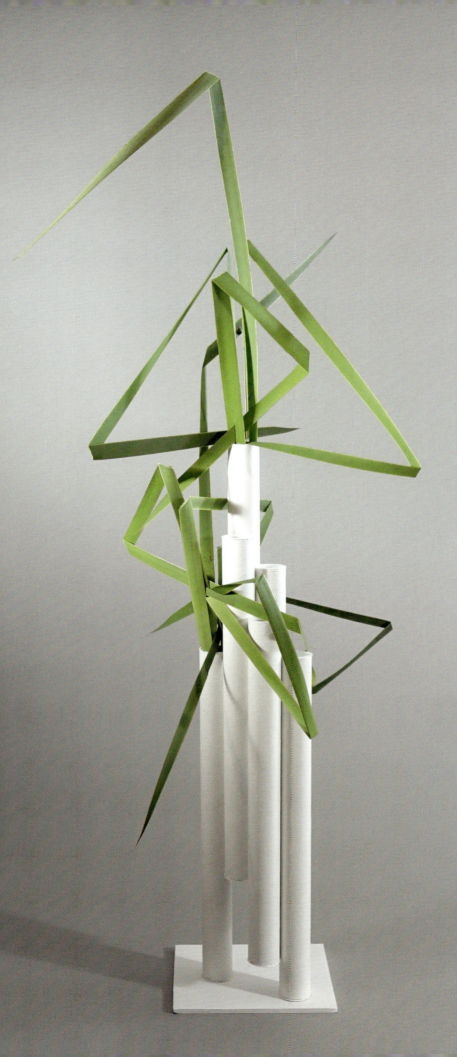

POINTED / ROUND

Angelika Mühlbauer
Germany

SOGETSU

STORMY / CALM

Chinara Munduzbaeva
Russia

SOGETSU

LIGHTNESS / GRAVITY

Ilse Neumayer
Austria

SOGETSU

BENT / STRAIGHT

Angelika Ochmann
Germany

SOGETSU

ROUGH / SMOOTH

Ohara Study Group Bologna
Italy

OHARA

DIFFIDENT / DARING

Mary Pearson
Northern Ireland

SOGETSU

ALL LEAVES / ALL FLOWERS

Margot C. Perez
Philippines

SOGETSU

GO UP / FALL DOWN

Do-Quyen Phan
France

SOGETSU

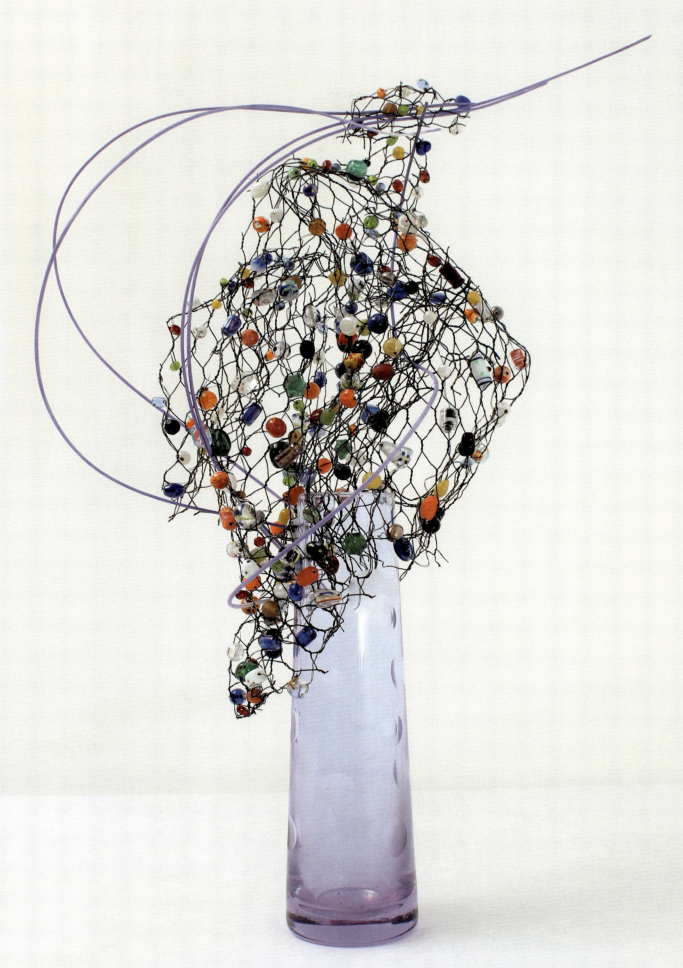

HOT / COLD

Lucia Pierelli
Italy

SOGETSU

175

DECAY / GROWTH

Hildegard Premer
Germany

IKENOBO

THE SPEAKER / THE AUDIENCE

Carmen Rothmayr
Switzerland

IKENOBO

SUMMER / WINTER

Lea Ruprecht
Switzerland

SOGETSU

COMMUNITY / SECLUSION

Roberta Santagostino
Italy

OHARA

FLUFFY / SPIKY

Larisa Sarycheva
Russia

SOGETSU

LITTLE / PLENTY

Henriëtte Schalk
the Netherlands

SOGETSU

CONFINEMENT /
FREEDOM

Renate Schnitzer
Austria

SOGETSU

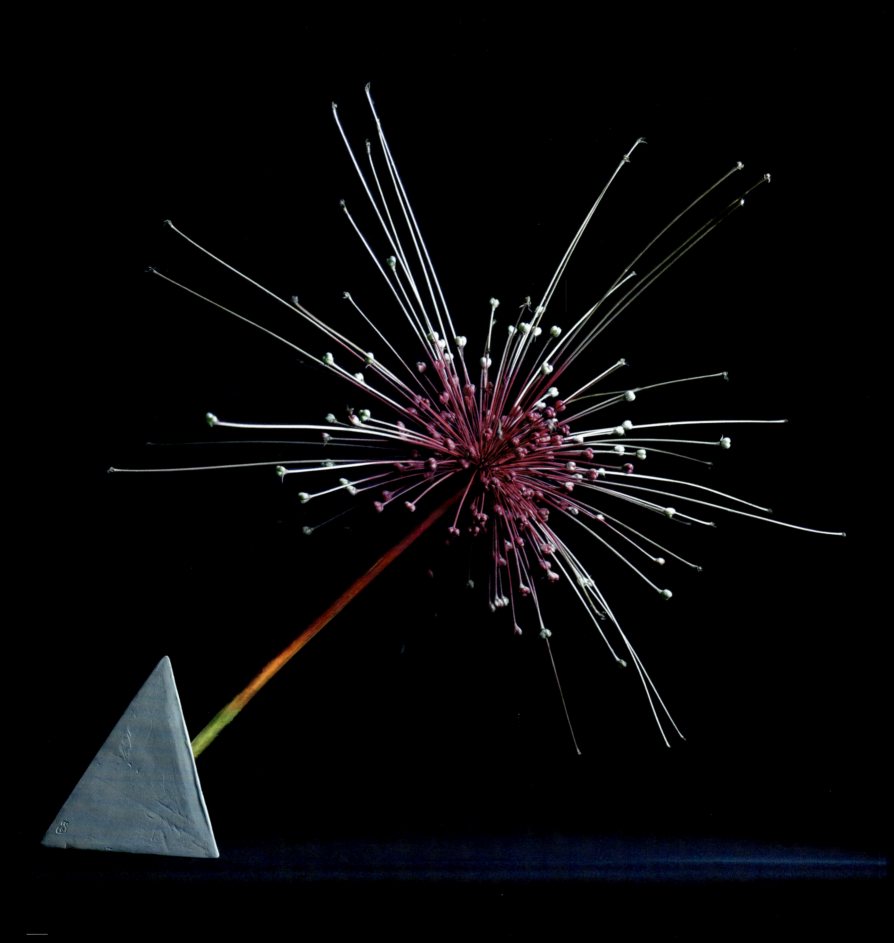

EXTROVERT / INTROVERT

Ekaterina Seehaus
Belgium

SOGETSU

SLUGGISH / NIMBLE

Greet Snoodijk
the Netherlands

SOGETSU

WAR / PEACE

Edeltraud Stiftner
Austria

SOGETSU

DEPARTURE / WITHDRAWAL

Elisabeth Streubel
Austria

SOGETSU

ADVANCED / BASIC

Emiko Suzuki
USA

IKENOBO

GATHERING / SCATTERING

Ryoka Tabuki
Germany

SOGETSU

PEACE / WAR

Haruko Takeichi
USA

SOGETSU

MATURITY / YOUTH

Larisa Telford
Australia

SOGETSU

WAR / PEACE

Inger Tribler
Denmark

SOGETSU

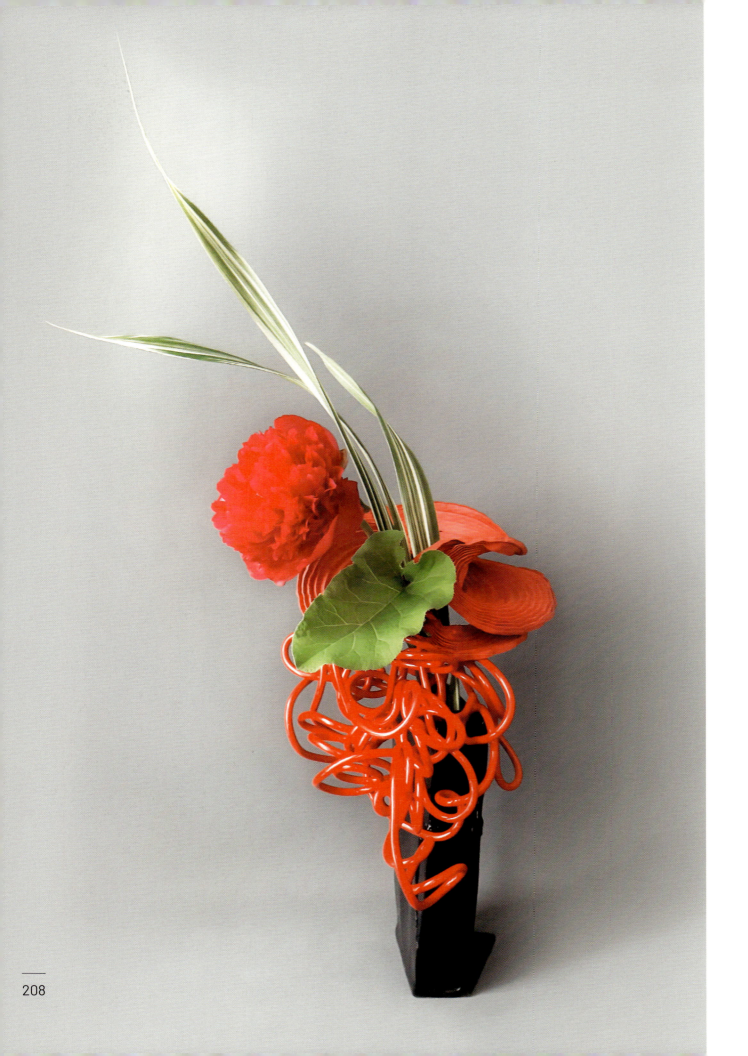

STRENGTH /
VULNERABILITY

Ingrid Truttmann
Austria

SOGETSU

STRONG / WEAK

Tatiana Tsoy
Russia

SOGETSU

DETERMINED / HESITATING

Siska Van de Steene
Belgium

SOGETSU

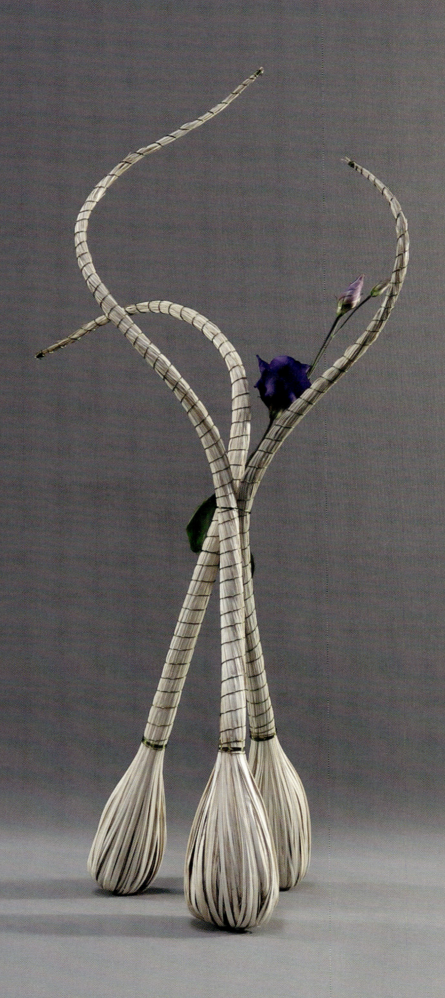

DEATH / LIFE

Rianne van der Steen
the Netherlands

SOGETSU/OHARA

DEATH / LIFE

Robert Van Hecke
Belgium

SOGETSU

BLACK / WHITE

Désirée van Vliet
the Netherlands

SOGETSU

INTROVERT / EXTROVERT

Lucia Veldeman
Belgium

SOGETSU

AIRY / MASSIVE

Anke Verhoeven
the Netherlands

SOGETSU

CLOSED / OPEN

Jeroen Vermaas
the Netherlands

ICHIYO

LOVE / HATE

Lily Vittot
France

ICHIYO

NEW / OLD

Ulrike Vogler
Germany

SOGETSU

FIRE / WATER

Anne-Riet Vugts
the Netherlands

SOGETSU

CONVEX / CONCAVE

Annelie Wagner
Germany

OHARA

CORNERED /
ROUND

Hilde Weichel
Germany

SOGETSU

CELESTIAL / TERRESTRIAL

Ursula Winand
Germany

SOGETSU

CONSTRAINED / FREE

Louise Worner
Spain

SOGETSU

ENERGETIC / RELAXED

Chung-chi Yu
Taiwan

IKENOBO

DESTROY / (RE)BUILD

Ursula Zembrot
Germany

SOGETSU

RIGIDITY / RESILIENCE

Lily Zhang
China

ICHIYO

PARTICIPANTS

Tory J. Lowitz p. 2
USA – SOGETSU
Photography: Tory J. Lowitz
Integrate/Disintegrate: wood, copper enamel, packing tape, cardboard, metal screws

Martha Bachmann p. 10-11
Switzerland – KAGEI ADACHI RYU
Photography: Dennis Savini, Marie-Madeleine Perler (portrait)
Chaos: Nicandra physalodes, Euonymus alatus, Digitaria sanguinalis
Harmony: Alcea ficifolia, Euonymus alatus

Denise Adriaensen p. 12-13
Belgium – OHARA
Photography: Denise Adriaensen
Young: Salix alba, aluminium
Old: Corylus avellana 'Contorta', corten steel

Rica Arai p. 14-15
France – SOGETSU
Photography: Kojima
Group: Taraxacum officinale
Individual: Taraxacum officinale

Paola Belfiore p. 16-17
Italy – SOGETSU
Photography: Paola Belfiore
Quietness: Pandanus, Plexiglas, rattan, Gerbera
Turmoil: bamboo root, copper wire

Atsuko Bersma p. 18-19
Belgium/Japan – SOGETSU
Portrait: Ben Huybrechts, René Bersma (portrait)
Masculine: Anthurium andraenum, Gerbera jamesonii, Platanus x hispanica, Sansevieria trifasciata
Feminine: Gypsophilia paniculata, Phalaenopsis

Ilse Beunen p. 20-21
Belgium – SOGETSU
Photography: Ben Huybrechts
Heavy: Helianthus, Hedera, Salix, Borago officinalis
Light: Tulipa

Alka Bhargava p. 22-23
USA – ICHIYO
Photography: Cory Piehowicz
Complex: Phyllostachys bambusoides, Corylus avellana, Gloriosa superba 'Rotschildiana', Clematis occidentalis
Simple: Phyllostachys bambusoides, Corylus avellana, Gloriosa superba 'Rotschildiana', Clematis occidentalis

Alie Bos-Praamstra p. 24-25
the Netherlands – SOGETSU
Photography: Wicher Bos
Captured: Gypsophila, paper
Free: Iris pseudacorus, Sambucus nigra, Japanese silk paper

Jean Brouwers p. 26-27
the Netherlands – SOGETSU
Photography: Désirée van Vliet
Amiable: Allium sativum var. ophioscorodon, Gloriosa superba, Lathyrus odoratus 'Prince of Orange', Oncidium flexuosum
Capricious: Lathyrus odoratus 'Prince of Orange', brown algae

Mieke Bruynooghe-Van Elslande p. 28-29
Belgium – SOGETSU
Photography: Kate Neels, Dirk Bruynooghe (portrait)
Geisha: Juncus effusus, Allium giganteum
Samourai: Allium giganteum, Aspidistra (leaf)

Brigitta Buse p. 30-31
Germany – SOGETSU
Photography: Felix Buse
Angular: Quercus rubra, Aspidistra elatior (sewn together with a button), Olea europea
Round: Salix caprea, Parthenocissus quinquefolia, Physalis alkekengi

Elizabeth Campbell p. 32-33
USA – ICHIYO
Photography: Patti Quinn Hill
Angular: Hydrangea, Anthurium leaf
Curved: Calla, bulrush

Christophe Capdeville p. 34-35
France – ICHIYO
Photography: Christophe Capdeville, Guillaume Le Fur (portrait)
Life: Cercis siliquastrum, Coronilla, Gerbera, Anemone, Narcissus jonquilla, Iris germanica, Hedera
Death: Allium schubertii, Lilium Chrysanthemum 'Santini', Hedera, Juncus, Phalaenopsis

Evangeline Y. Cheng p. 36-37
Philippines – SOGETSU
Photography: Julius Ivan Yang Tan, Jack Kenaz Cheng (portrait)
Curved: Zantedeschia elliottiana, Begonia chloroneura, Clitoria ternatea (vine)
Angular: Typha angustifolia, Curcuma zedoaria

Els Claes p. 38-39
Belgium – IKENOBO
Photography: Els Claes
Defiant: Hemerocallis sp.
Submissive: Fuchsia magellanica 'Tricolor', Allium sphaerocephalon, Begonia 'Little Brother Montgomery'

Zilá Da Costa Raymundo p. 40-41
Brazil – SOGETSU
Photography: Robson Cesco
Decay: Helianthus annuus (dry), Musa (dry banana leaf)
Perkiness: Musa (banana leaf), Gloriosa rotschildiana

Elin Dahlin p. 42-43
Sweden – SOGETSU
Photography: Rod Westwood
Connect: Trachycarpus, Citrullus lanatus, Solanum lycopersicum
Separate: Dracaena trifasciata, Citrullus lanatus, Solanum lycopersicum

Anna Maria De Carvalho p. 44-45
Switzerland – MISHO-RYU
Photography: Elisa De Carvalho (portrait), Ursina Früh
Extrovert: Delphinium belladonna 'Völkerfrieden', Eustoma grandiflorum, Dianthus barbatus 'Green Trick'
Introvert: Delphinium belladonna 'Völkerfrieden', Eustoma grandiflorum, Dianthus barbatus 'Green Trick', Xanthorrhoea australis

Wil de Theije p. 46-47
the Netherlands – SOGETSU
Photography: Wil Oortman
Dynamic: Fallopia sachalinensis (bleached), metal cube 1 x 1 x 1 m, 2 coloured balls
Static: Fallopia sachalinensis (bleached), metal cube 45 x 45 x 45 cm, 1 coloured ball

Angelika Denig p. 48-49
Germany – SOGETSU
Photography: Ayako Graefe, Franz-Josef Denig (portrait)
Angular: Zantedeschia, Aspidistra
Round: Centaurea cyanus, Diplopterygium pinnatum

Brigitte Depienne p. 50-51
Belgium – SOGETSU
Photography: Annika Ingelaere, Daniel Depienne (portrait)
Freed: Hosta plantaginea, Allium polyanthum
Locked-up: Hosta plantaginea, Allium polyanthum

Claire Devleminckx p. 52-53
Belgium – SOGETSU
Photography: Ekaterina Seehaus
Life: Hydrangea, Hosta
Death: Hydrangea, Hosta

Rita Dollberg p. 54-55
Germany – SOGETSU
Photography: Marion Hogl, Lukas Loske (portrait)
Meat Lover: Celosia cristata, Chryanthemum, Astilbe arendsii, Osmunda regalis
Vegetarian: Anethum graveolens, Allium sativum

Christine Donck Guelton p. 56-57
USA – SOGETSU
Photography: Ben Huybrechts
Unraveled: copper wire, origami paper, Aeonium gomerense
Intertwined: reed, Dahlia, Typha

Damien Dufour p. 58-59
France – OHARA
Photography: Damien Dufour
With: driftwood, Solidago, Canna indica, Fucus serratus, shell
Without: Iris pallida variegata, Fucus serratus, Chrysanthemum

Christl Dullenkopf p. 60-61
Germany – SOGETSU
Photography: Christl Dullenkopf
Confined: dry branch, Primula vulgaris
Free: Rosa canina

Valerie Eccleston p. 62-63
USA – ICHIYO
Photography: Elena Makarova
Hello: Helianthus, Veronica, Micanthus sinensis, Matricaria
Goodbye: Helianthus, Sorberia sorbifolia, Corylus avellana 'Contorta'

Alexander Evans p. 64-65
Australia – SOGETSU
Photography: Alexander Evans
Absorption: Chrysanthemum x morifolium, Papaver nudicaule (poppy), Gahnia grandis (sword grass)
Reflection: Papaver nudicaule, Gahnia grandis (sword grass)

Huda Fallaha p. 66-67
Jordan – SOGETSU
Photography: Simon Balian
Simple: Hibiscus syriacus, Hedera helix (dry and coloured branches)
Complicated: Hibiscus syriacus, Eustoma exaltatum subsp. Russellianum, Hedera helix (dry and coloured branches)

Yi-Li Fang p. 68-69
Taiwan – IKENOBO
Photography: Fang Yi-Li
Timeless beauty: Lotus, Nuphar shimadae 'Hayata' (yellow water lily), Iris laevigata, Iris ochroleuca
Wabi Sabi: Lotus, Gloriosa, Scirpus tabernaemontani 'Zebrinus'

Farah Fazrina Rauf p. 70-71
Malaysia – SOGETSU
Photography: Farah Fazrina
Culture: Allium hollandicum, Ranunculus asiaticus, Pandanus veitchii
Nature: Enkianthus perulatus, Iris ensata Murakumo, Iris ensata shokkou, Astilbe arendsii, Clematis socialis

Esther Feucht p. 72-73
Switzerland – MISHO-RYU
Photography: Esther Feucht, Foto Rüti (portrait)
Fresh: Acer palmatum
Noble: Larix

Maude Freymond Wanner p. 74-75
Australia – SOGETSU
Photography: Yves Burdet
Emerge: Triticum aestivum, Loeskeobryum brevirostre (moss), black pebbles
Decline: Heuchera sanguinea, Cotinus coggygria, Fagus salvaticus

Ursina Früh p. 76-77
Switzerland – MISHO-RYU
Photography: Ursina Früh, Fotostudio Kamber (portrait)
Liquid: Hosta (leaves), Philodendron Xanadu (leaves), Calla
Solid: Hosta (leaves), Philodendron Xanadu (leaves), Calla

Lucienne Girardbille p. 78-79
France – IKENOBO
Photography: Lucienne Girardbille
Frivolous: Geranium sylvaticum, Iridaceae, Foeniculum vulgare, Chamaecyparis variegata
Serious: Typha latifolia, Zantedeschia

Irene Gomulka p. 80-81
USA – SOGETSU
Photography: Irene Gomulka
Past: Protea cynaroides, Strelitzia Nicolai, self-made container
Present: Protea cynaroides, Strelitzia Nicolai, self-made container

Ayako Graefe p. 82-83
Germany – SOGETSU
Photography: Ayako Graefe, Volker Graefe (portrait)
Open: Monstera deliciosa, Alchemilla mollis
Closed: Monstera deliciosa, Alchemilla mollis

Herbert Grünsteidl p. 84-85
Austria – SOGETSU
Photography: Bettina Grünsteidl-Miller
Vigorous: Heliconia vellerigera, Furcraea foetida
Fragile: Albizia julibrissin, Acer palmatum 'Seiryu',

Fatima Hanke p. 86-87
Germany – SOGETSU
Photography: Wilfried Hanke
Breakable/Unbreakable: Gerbera, Styrofoam, silver wire
Bright/Dark: Hydrangea, branches (painted black and white)

Mechtild Hartz-Riemann p. 88-89
Germany – SOGETSU
Photography: Mechtild Hartz-Riemann, Mrs. Mertens (portrait)
Complete: Carpinus betulus (coloured), Gerbera
Broken: Carpinus betulus (coloured), Gerbera

Edelgard Herwald p. 90-91
Germany – SOGETSU
Photography: Arnold Engel
Round: Darmera peltata, Hydrangea arborescens
Angular: Darmera peltata, Zea leaves, Zinnia, Asteracea, Bamboo sticks

Esther Hoogland p. 92-93
the Netherlands – SOGETSU
Photography: Frank Kho
Young: Ptelea trifoliata (seeds)
Old: Gunnera (dried leaf), Tulipa

Marilyn Hoskins p. 94-95
USA – ICHIYO
Photography: Lindsey Carpenter Hoskins
Love: Anthurium, Zantedeschia aethiopica, Betula (branch), Monstera deliciosa, Allium, Asteraceae
Hate: Protea cynaroides, Protea leucospermum, Chrysantemum Disbud, Allium, Trifoliate branch, Philodendron bipinnatifidum

Jeanne Houlton p. 96-97
USA – ICHIYO
Photography: Jeanne Houlton
First sun of summer: Oncidium, Bambusa ventricosa, Manzanita
Last light of winter: Coryllus avellana 'Contorta', Strelitzia nicolai

Misha Huurman (†) p. 98-99
the Netherlands – SOGETSU
Photography: Rita van der Werf, Désirée van Vliet (portrait)
Joy: Gypsophila muralis, Gerbera 'Insider'
Sadness: Gypsophila muralis, coloured wood

Ikenobo Swiss Central Chapter: Shunzuen Suzue Rother-Nakaya and Chaoyu Du p. 100-101
Switzerland – IKENOBO
Photography: Chaoyu Du
Day: Crocosmia japonica, Platycodon, Hypericum, Dendromecon rigida, grass
Night: Platycodon, Gypsophila paniculata, Dendromecon rigida, Hypericum, Heuchera (leaf)

Mit Ingelaere-Brandt p. 102-103
Belgium – SOGETSU
Photography: Annika Ingelaere
Sunny side: Strelitzia
Shadow side: Strelitzia

Elaine Jo p. 104-105
USA – ICHIYO
Photography: Elaine Jo, Patti Quinn Hill (portrait)
Upward movement: Anthurium andraeanum, Dianthus 'Solomio', Amaryllis (green leaf)
Downward movement: Arctostaphylos manzanita, Paeonia suffruticosa, Alstroemeria, Nandina domestica

Gisela Jost p. 106-107
Germany – Sogetsu
Photography: Gisela Jost
Self-confident: Allium 'Millennium', wood, ceramic container, leaf
Unsure: Paeonia officinalis (flowers and leaves), red chicken wire, black glass container

Elena Karetko p. 108-109
Russia – SOGETSU
Photography: Alexey Popov, Andrey Ostapenko (portrait)
Soul: Hosta leaves; Allium schubertii, paper
Body: Tree bark, flexigrass, plastic wire, metal stand (own design)

Irene Kho-Chen p. 110-111
the Netherlands – OHARA
Photography: Frank Kho
Earth: Cornus sanguinea, Viburnum, Heracleum, Sanguisorba officinalis, Athyrium
Heaven: Heracleum, Cotinus coggygria, white mitsumata

Elena Kilchevskaya p. 112-113
Russia – SOGETSU
Photography: Alexei Popov, Ekaterina Grashenkova (portrait)
Dry: Ammodendron, Monstera
Wet: Lupinus, Papaver

Antje Klatt p. 114-115
Germany – SOGETSU
Photography: Reinhard Wirtz
Freedom: Crateagus (dry branch), Gloriosa superba
Oppression: Crateagus (dry branch), washi paper

Iryna Korol Latorre p. 116-117
USA – ICHIYO
Photography: Elena Makarova
Day: Lavandula angustifolia, Iris (leaves), Petunia, Streptocarpus saxorum
Night: Spathiphyllum wallisii, Monarda, Aspidistra elatior 'Milky Way'

Nicole Kruimel-Rosselle p. 118-119
the Netherlands – SOGETSU
Photography: Nicole Kruimel – Rosselle
Heavy: Larix, Quercus, Pseudotsuga menziesii
Light: packaging material

Bodil Kuhn p. 120-121
Switzerland – IKENOBO
Photography: Bodil Kuhn
Strong: Daucus carota, Rosa, Hypericum
Tender: Daucus carota, Rosa, Hypericum

Iris Kuhn p. 122-123
Austria – ICHIYO
Photography: Erwin Kuhn
Loneliness: Agapanthus
Secureness: Agapanthus

Urana Kuular p. 124-125
Russia – SOGETSU
Photography: Alexander Gorishniy
Connect: Papaver, Eucalyptus bark
Separate: Papaver, Eucalyptus bark

Kathy LaDuke p. 126-127
USA – ICHIYO
Photography: Kathy LaDuke
Fire: Serenoa repens, Hamelia patens, Nandina domestica 'Seika', lime rocks
Ice: Hydrangea macrophylla, Gypsophila paniculata, Limonium latifolium

Tanja Lähteenmäki p. 128-129
Finland – SOGETSU
Photography: Antti Lähteenmäki
Loud: electrical wire, painted wooden sticks, Rosa, Cordyline
Silent: Anthriscus sylvestris, Trifolium pratense

Marcia Lamrock p. 130-131
Australia – SOGETSU
Photography: Dale McKeon
Confinement: Euphorbia wulfenii
Freedom: Euphorbia wulfenii

Marta Lanfranco p. 132-133
Italy – WAFU KAI
Photography: Marta Lanfranco, Luca Simoncello (portrait)
Yin: Cotinus coggygria, Hydrangea macrophylla (Thunb.), Diervilla sessilifolia Buckley
Yang: Wisteria sinensis (Sims), Trachycarpus fortunei, Edgeworthia tomentosa (Thunb.), Hemerocallis fulva (L.)

Hélène Lanz p. 134-135
Germany – SOGETSU
Photography: Hélène Lanz, Alexander Vogl (portrait)
Light: Aesculus parviflora, highly weathered tree stump
Shadow: Celosia argentea var. cristata, Dianthus barbatus, Fraxinus excelsior (bark)

Ivy Le Maguer p. 136-137
France – IKENOBO
Photography: Detlef Ahlers
Classical: Hydrangea macrophylla, Iris pseudocorus, Canna coccinea, Stipa gigantea, Crepis vesicaria, Parthenocissus tricuspidata, Pinus
Modern: Allium gigantea, Actinidia deliciosa, Photinia japonica, Euonymus japonica, Ilex aquifolium, Iridaceae

Zoo-Lan Lee-Rötter p. 138-139
Germany – OHARA
Photography: Dennis Prahl
Modesty: Polystichum, Bellis perennis
Pride: Punica granatum, Phalaenopsis, Hydrangea, Nelumbo

Verdy Leung p. 140-141
Hong Kong – IKENOBO
Photography: Verdy Leung, Zero Yiu
Old: Iris laevigata
Young: Iris laevigata, Nuphar shimadai

Gisele Leuther p. 142-143
Germany – OHARA
Photography: Annelie Wagner, Gisela Leuther (portrait)
North (Europe): Limonium, Smoke grass, Agapanthus, reindeer horn
South (Europe): Citrus sinensis, Platycodon, Heuchera, Limonium

Hedda Lintner p. 144-145
Germany – SOGETSU
Photography: Helene Lanz, Friedrich Jäck
Destroyed: Malus domestica
Recreated: Triticum, Papaver rhoeas

Pat Mackie p. 146-147
Australia – SOGETSU
Photography: Pat Mackie
Yang: Muehlenbeckia platyclada (green), Iris, Vanda
Yin: Strelitzia nicolai, rusty pipe

Regula Maier p. 148-149
Switzerland – MISHO
Photography: Ursina Früh, Klaus Pfisterer (portrait)
Left: Aspidistra
Right: Aspidistra

Milla Mäkinen p. 150-151
Finland – SOGETSU
Photography: Milla Mäkinen
Sharp: Dianthus, Gypsophila
Soft: Dianthus, Dendranthema, Gypsophila

Rumiko Manako p. 152-153
Japan/France – IKENOBO
Photography: Rumiko Manako
Motion: Narcissus, Cyclamen, Iris japonica
Stillness: Narcissus

Inès Massin p. 154-155
Switzerland – SOGETSU
Photography: Yves Burdet
Bliss: Asparagus, Edgeworthia chrysantha (mitsumata), Acacia dealbata
Anguish: Achillea millefolium, metallic thread, black wood

Gerda Matthees p. 156-157
Belgium – SOGETSU
Photography: Guy Dierckens
Compact: Photinia 'Red Robin', Anthurium
Airy: Ficus religiosa (skeletonized), copper wire

Angelika Mühlbauer   p. 158-159
Germany – SOGETSU
Photography: Ayako Graefe,
Angelika Mühlbauer (portrait)
Pointed: Typhaceae
Round: Dianthus barbatus 'Green Trick', red Dianthus

Chinara Munduzbaeva   p. 160-161
Russia – SOGETSU
Photography: Alexey Popov
Stormy: Iris (flowers and leaves)
Calm: Iris (flowers and leaves)

Ilse Neumayer   p. 162-163
Austria – SOGETSU
Photography: Helmut Neumayer
Gravity: Parthenocissus quinquefolia, granite
Lightness: Parthenocissus tricuspidata, pebbles

Angelika Ochmann   p. 164-165
Germany – SOGETSU
Photography: Ayako Graefe,
Angelika Mühlbauer (portrait)
Bent: Allium sativum, Phacelia tanacetifolia
Straight: Allium porrum, Allium 'Red Mohican', Allium sphaerocephalon, Allium cernum, Allium 'Hair'

Ohara Study Group Bologna   p. 166-167
Italy – OHARA
Photography: Margherita Cecchini
Rough: Acer japonicum, Cocos nucifera, Cynaria cardunculus, white paper
Smooth: Aspidistra, Anthurium, coal

Mary Pearson   p. 168-169
Northern Ireland – SOGETSU
Photography: Ben Huybrechts (daring), Mary Pearson (portrait, diffident)
Diffident: Prunus, Rudbeckia hirta
Daring: Cotinus coggygria, Juncus

Margot C. Perez   p. 170-171
Philippines – SOGETSU
Photography: Julius Ivan Yang Tan, Joseph C. Perez
All leaves: Anthurium 'Renaissance', Asparagus setaceus, Yucca elephantipes
All flowers: Lagerstroemia indica, Heliconia chartacea, Gerbera jamesonii

Do-Quyen Phan   p. 172-173
France – SOGETSU
Photography: Do-Quyen Phan
Go up: Sedum reflexum, Clarkia amoena
Fall down: Sanguisorba obtusa, Dianthus caryophyllus

Lucia Pierelli   p. 174-175
Italy – SOGETSU
Photography: Lucia Pierelli
Hot: rattan strings, acryl (plastic)
Cold: rattan strings, wire mesh and coloured glass beads

Hildegard Premer   p. 176-177
Germany – IKENOBO
Photography: Anna Schamschula
Decay: Anthurium (leaf), Clematis, Chrysanthemum, Calamagrostis acutiflora
Growth: Salix caprea, Pseudosasa japonica, Mahonia aquifolia

Carmen Rothmayr   p. 178-179
Switzerland – IKENOBO
Photography: Carmen Rothmayr
The Speaker: Coryllus contorta (painted black), Cyperus, Craspedia globosa, Kalanchoe blossfeldiana
The Audience: Coryllus contorta (painted black), Vriesea 'Astrid', Helleborus niger, Oxipetalum, Argyranthemum frutescens

Lea Ruprecht   p. 180-181
Switzerland – SOGETSU
Photography: Lea Ruprecht, Hannu Ruprecht (portrait)
Summer: Lathyrus odoratus, Tagetes patula, Campanula carpatica
Winter: Aspidistra (dried leaves), wood shavings, plexi glass

Roberta Santagostino   p. 182-183
Italy – OHARA
Photography: Roberta Santagostino
Community: Muscari armeniacum, Camellia japonica, Acer palmatum 'Dissectum'
Seclusion: Muscari armeniacum, Camellia japonica, Acer palmatum 'Dissectum'

Larisa Sarycheva   p. 184-185
Russia – SOGETSU
Photography: Tatiana Rodionova, Polina Almaeva (portrait)
Fluffy: Taraxacum
Spiky: Crateagus (painted), Acanthus

Henriëtte Schalk   p. 186-187
the Netherlands – SOGETSU
Photography: Toke van Bragt
Little: Cornus sericea, one piece of ceramic
Plenty: Cornus alba, pieces of ceramic

Renate Schnitzer p. 188-189
Austria – SOGETSU
Photography: Renate Schnitzer
Confinement: Thuja occidentalis 'Brabant', Allium sphaerocephalon
Freedom: Spiraea nipponica, Eustoma grandiflorum

Ekaterina Seehaus p. 190-191
Belgium – SOGETSU
Photography: Ekaterina Seehaus, Cédric Gypen (portrait)
Extrovert: Allium schubertii
Introvert: Paeonia, Hosta

Greet Snoodijk p. 192-193
the Netherlands – SOGETSU
Photography: Frank Kho, Fotowereld Utrecht (portrait)
Sluggish: Buxus, Betula pendula
Nimble: Buxus, Betula pendula, Buddleja

Edeltraud Stiftner p. 194-195
Austria – SOGETSU
Photography: Roman Stiftner
War: Allium, Acacia cornigera, red plastic rods, two spherical ceramic vases
Peace: Anthurium, Gypsophila paniculata, plastic strap, two handcrafted conical ceramic vases

Elisabeth Streubel p. 196-197
Austria – SOGETSU
Photography: Oskar Streubel
Departure: Salix sepulcralis, Alstroemeria
Withdrawal: Salix sepulcralis, Clematis

Emiko Suzuki p. 198-199
USA – IKENOBO
Photography: Emiko Suzuki
Advanced: Hydrangea, Iris orientalis, Daucus carota
Basic: Hydrangea, Iris orientalis, Heliconia, Asparagus densiflorus, Polygonatum odoratum var., Eustoma, Polystichum acrostichoides

Ryoka Tabuki p. 200-201
Germany – SOGETSU
Photography: Ryoka Tabuki, Wolfgang Denk (portrait)
Gathering: Allium
Scattering: Allium

Haruko Takeichi p. 202-203
USA – SOGETSU
Photography: Hilow Fumihiro Hirota
Peace: Hydrangea, Lathyrus odoratus, Salix matsudana
War: Poncirus torifoliata, Asparagus virgatus, Bassia scoparia, Zantedeschia, Cotinus coggygria

Larisa Telford p. 204-205
Australia – SOGETSU
Photography: Vladimir Tsyskin
Maturity: Persimmon, Acer palmatum, Eucalyptus camaldulensis
Youth: Citrus x paradisi (grapefruit), Dendrobium, Philodendron gloriosum (leaves)

Inger Tribler p. 206-207
Denmark – SOGETSU
Photography: Inger Tribler, Bjarne Leth Nielsen
War: Iris sibirica, Robinia pseudoacacia (coloured branches)
Peace: Cornus florida f. rubra, Edgeworthia chrysantha (coloured mitsumata)

Ingrid Truttmann p. 208-209
Austria – SOGETSU
Photography: Ingrid Truttmann, Lisa Truttmann (portrait)
Strength: Paeonia, Phormium, weed, red Japanese wire, red folded paper, black handmade container
Vulnerability: Aspidistra, Carduus, acupuncture needles, handmade container

Tatiana Tsoy p. 210-211
Russia – SOGETSU
Photography: Alexey Popov
Strong: Quercus (old oak stump), Arctium leaves
Weak: Avanella flexuosa, Freesia refracta

Siska Van de Steene p. 212-213
Belgium – SOGETSU
Photography: Koenraad Maes
Determined: Arbutus unedo, Gerbera, Hosta
Hesitating: Arbutus unedo, Gerbera

Rianne van der Steen p. 214-215
the Netherlands – SOGETSU/OHARA
Photography: Rita van der Werf
Death: Xerophyllum tenax, Eustoma russellianum
Life: Xerophyllum tenax, Eustoma russellianum

Rita van der Werf p. 216-217
the Netherlands – SOGETSU
Photography: Rita van der Werf
Past: Calla, rusted iron
Present: Phormium, aluminium tubes

Robert Van Hecke p. 218-219
Belgium – SOGETSU
Photography: Jean-Pierre Drubbels
Death: Anthurium, Populus nigra
Life: Tulipa 'Extra Parrot', Prunus avium

Désirée van Vliet p. 220-221
the Netherlands – SOGETSU
Photography: Désirée van Vliet, Jan van Vliet (portrait)
Black: Astilboides tabularis (dried and coloured), Pseudotsuga menziesii (bark), Iris pseudacorus (coloured leaves), Craspedia globosa (dried and coloured)
White: Astilboides tabularis (dried and coloured), Pseudotsuga menziesii (bark), Iris pseudacorus (coloured leaves), Craspedia globosa (dried and coloured)

Lucia Veldeman p. 222-223
Belgium – SOGETSU
Photography: Lucia Veldeman
Introvert: Chrysanthemum
Extrovert: Helianthus annuus

Anke Verhoeven p. 224-225
the Netherlands – SOGETSU
Photography: Désirée van Vliet
Airy: Perspex, chicken wire, paper, jute
Massive: Phalaenopsis, Musa (leaf), Betula (bark), chicken wire, paper, jute

Jeroen Vermaas p. 226-227
the Netherlands – ICHIYO
Photography: Jeroen Vermaas
Closed: Asplenium 'Osaka', Scabiosa caucasica, Veronica spicata, Ichiyo glass container
Open: Asplenium 'Osaka', Anthum graveolens, Matricaria, Ichiyo ceramic container

Lily Vittot p. 228-229
France – ICHIYO
Photography: Julien Chinot
Love: Corylus avellana 'Contorta', Hydrangea, Ornithogalum, Spiraea
Hate: Prunus cerasifera, Zantedeschia, Crocosmia 'Lucifer'

Ulrike Vogler p. 230-231
Germany – SOGETSU
Photography: Ulrike Vogler, Renate Murawski (portrait)
New: Fragaria vesca
Old: Fragaria vesca

Anne-Riet Vugts p. 232-233
the Netherlands – SOGETSU
Photography: Anne-Riet Vugts, Peter Luyten (portrait)
Fire: Betulus utilis, plastic rod
Water: Alga laminaria, Aspidistra

Annelie Wagner p. 234-235
Germany – OHARA
Photography: Annelie Wagner
Convex: Pinus (bark), Mangifera indica (mango)
Concave: Pinus mugo, Pine (bark)

Hilde Weichel p. 236-237
Germany – SOGETSU
Photography: Hilde Weichel, Ursula Worms (portrait)
Cornered: Allium 'Miami', Epimedium x perralchicum, rusty metal
Round: Allium 'Purple Sensation'

Ursula Winand p. 238-239
Germany – SOGETSU
Photography: Werner Moehler
Celestial: Agave, Allium, Poncirus trifoliata
Terrestrial: Allium giganteum, Trachycarpus, Poncirus trifoliata

Louise Worner p. 240-241
Spain – SOGETSU
Photography: Ben Huybrechts, Shane Worner (portrait)
Constrained: Craspedia globosa, Xanthorrhoea, copper wire
Free: Xanthorrhoea, seed pods (dried and drilled), copper wire

Chung-chi Yu p. 242-243
Taiwan – IKENOBO
Photography: Chung-chi Yu
Energetic: Prunus lannesiana wils. 'Gioiko', Scirpus tabernaemontani, Clematis florida Thunb.
Relaxed: Magnolia liliflora, Scirpus tabernaemontani, Philodendron

Ursula Zembrot p. 244-245
Germany – SOGETSU
Photography: Christl Dullenkopf, Gunnar Meier (portrait)
Destroy: Alnus glutinosa
(Re)build: Lilium longiflorum, Phoenix canariensis

Lily Zhang p. 246-247
China – ICHIYO
Photography: Philip Alien Wu, Jason Zou (portrait)
Rigidity: Bamboo, Heliconia bihai
Resilience: Bamboo, Bamboo strips, Protea cynaroides

Advisory team

Atsuko Bersma

Els Claes

Esther Hoogland

Mit Ingelaere-Brandt

Ivy Le Maguer

Jeroen Vermaas

Art director

Jaak Van Damme

Final editing

Katrien Van Moerbeke

Layout

www.groupvandamme.eu

Published by

Stichting Kunstboek bv

Legeweg 165

8020 Oostkamp

Belgium

info@stichtingkunstboek.com

www.stichtingkunstboek.com

ISBN 978-90-5856-696-6

D/2023/6407/01

NUR 421

Printed in the EU

All rights reserved. No part of this book may be reproduced, stored in a database or a retrieval system, or transmitted, in any form or by any means, electronically, mechanically, by print, microfilm or otherwise without prior permission from the Publisher.

While Stichting Kunstboek Publishers makes every effort possible to publish full and correct credits for each work included in this volume, sometimes errors of omission or commission may occur. For this Stichting Kunstboek Publishers is most regretful, but hereby must disclaim any liability.

© Stichting Kunstboek 2023